Kirklees

Cultural Services Headquarters

D1486482

BELOVED HYMNS

CONTENTS

— PIANO LEVEL —
LATE ELEMENTARY/EARLY INTERMEDIATE
(HLSPL LEVEL 3-4)

ISBN 0-634-06830-X

HAL•LEONARD® CORPORATION

7777 W. BLUEMOUND RD. P.O. BOX 13819 MILWAUKEE, WI 53213

In Australia Contact:
Hal Leonard Australia Pty. Ltd.
22 Taunton Drive   P.O. Box 5130
Cheltenham East, 3192   Victoria, Australia
Email: ausadmin@halleonard.com

250 547 560

www.halleonard.com
Visit Phillip at
www.phillipkeveren.com

ALL HAIL THE POWER OF JESUS' NAME

Words by EDWARD PERRONET
Altered by JOHN RIPPON
Music by OLIVER HOLDEN
Arranged by Phillip Keveren

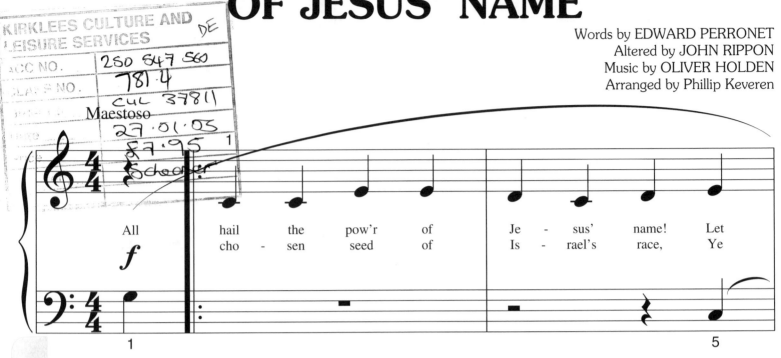

3

COME, THOU FOUNT
OF EVERY BLESSING

Words by ROBERT ROBINSON
Music by *The Sacred Harp*
Arranged by Phillip Keveren

5

BE STILL, MY SOUL

Words by KATHARINA VON SCHLEGEL
Translated by KATHARINA VON SCHLEGEL
Music by JEAN SIBELIUS
Arranged by Phillip Keveren

With dignity

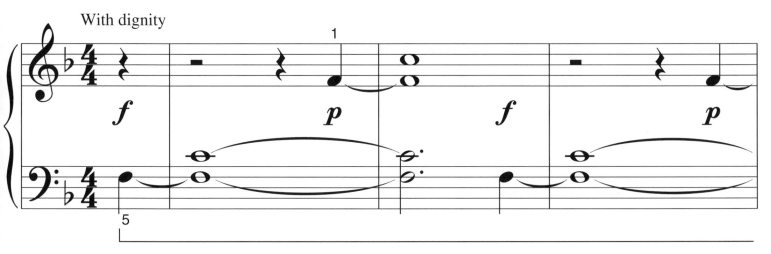

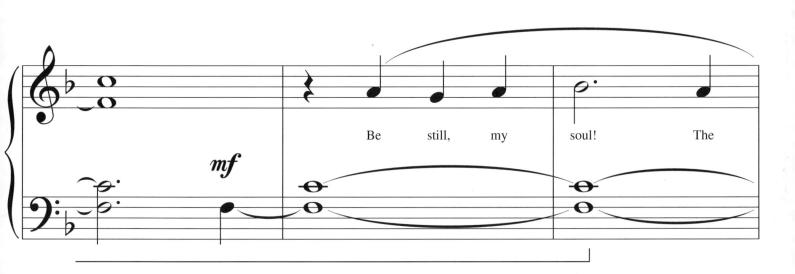

Be still, my soul! The

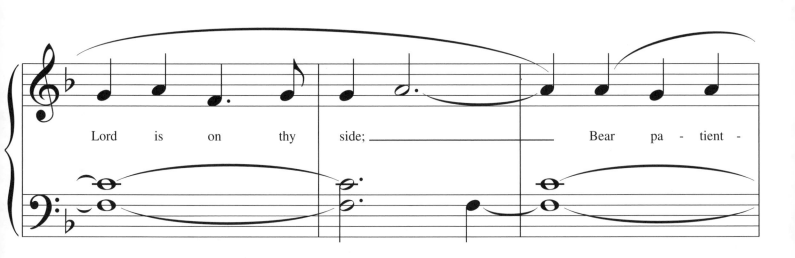

Lord is on thy side; Bear pa - tient -

9

BE THOU MY VISION

Traditional Irish
Translated by MARY E. BYRNE
Arranged by Phillip Keveren

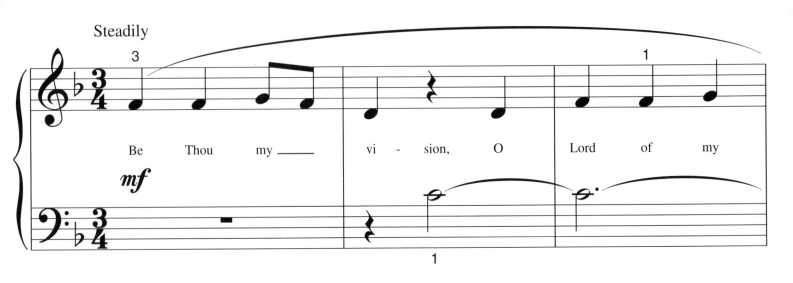

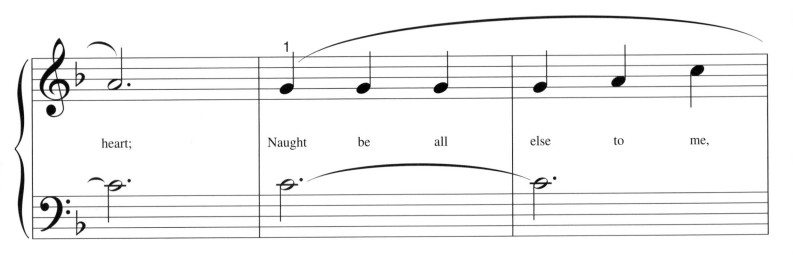

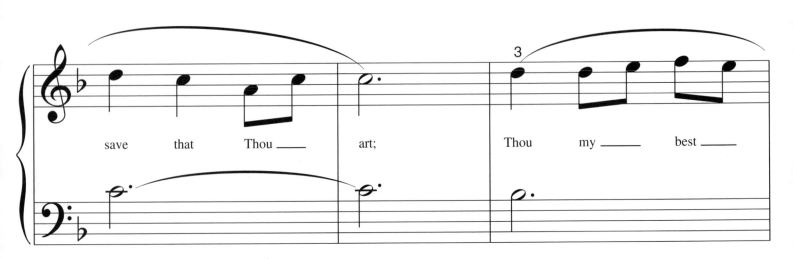

son, _____

Thou in me

p

dwell - ing, and _____ I with Thee one.

f *rit. e dim.*

pp

Very slow, freely

ppp

8vb - - - - - - - - - - - - - - - - - -

14

THE CHURCH'S ONE FOUNDATION

Words by SAMUEL JOHN STONE
Music by SAMUEL SEBASTIAN WESLEY
Arranged by Phillip Keveren

COME, THOU LONG-EXPECTED JESUS

Words by CHARLES WESLEY
Music by ROWLAND HUGH PRICHARD
Arranged by Phillip Keveren

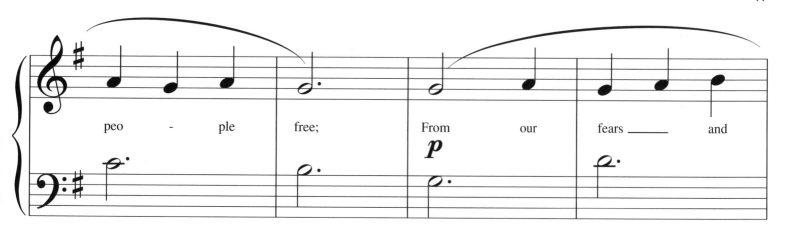

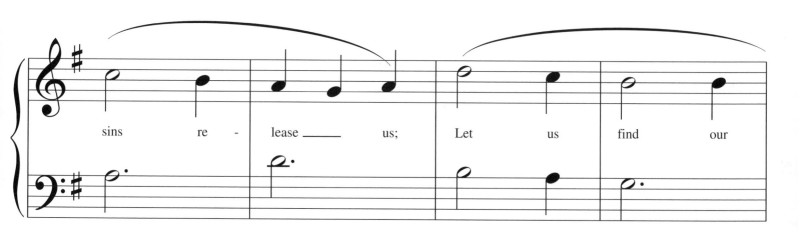

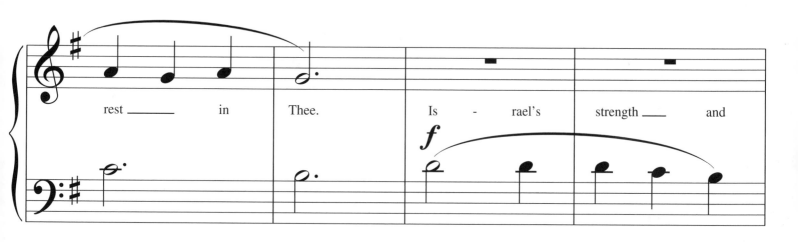

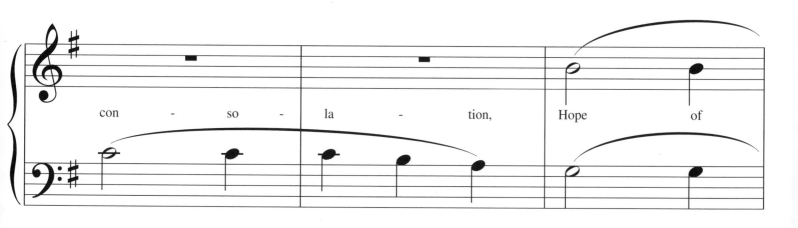

18

FAIREST LORD JESUS

Words from *Munster Gesangbuch*
Verse 4 by JOSEPH A. SEISS
Music from *Schlesische Volkslieder*
Arranged by Phillip Keveren

Peacefully, freely

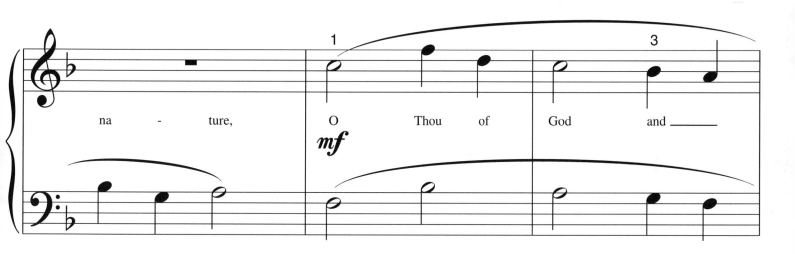

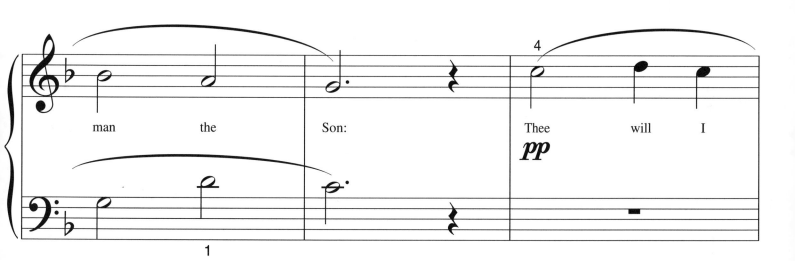

NEARER, MY GOD, TO THEE

Words by SARAH F. ADAMS
Based on Genesis 28:10-22
Music by LOWELL MASON
Arranged by Phillip Keveren

Prayerfully

Near - er, my God, to Thee, Near - er to
Though like the wan - der - er, The sun gone

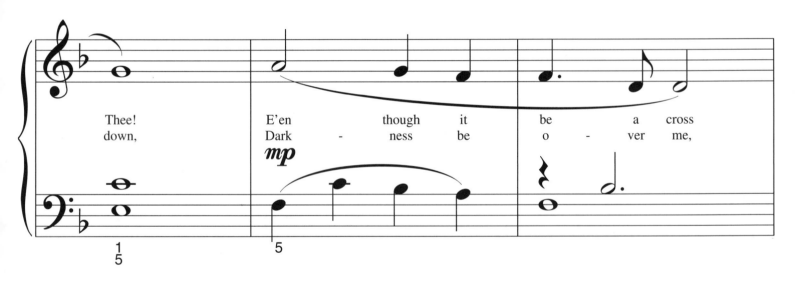

Thee! E'en though it be a cross
down, Dark - ness it be o - ver me,

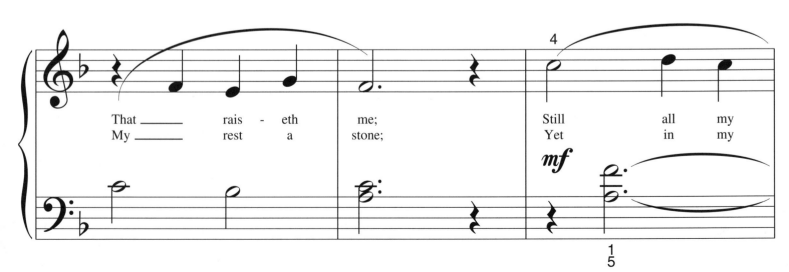

That ___ rais - eth me; Still all my
My ___ rest a stone; Yet in my

23

HE LEADETH ME

Words by JOSEPH H. GILMORE
Music by WILLIAM B. BRADBURY
Arranged by Phillip Keveren

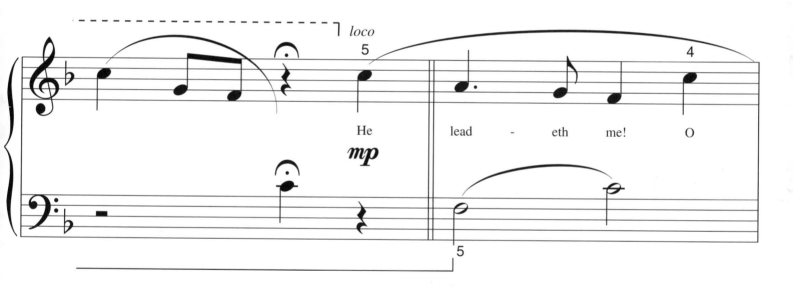

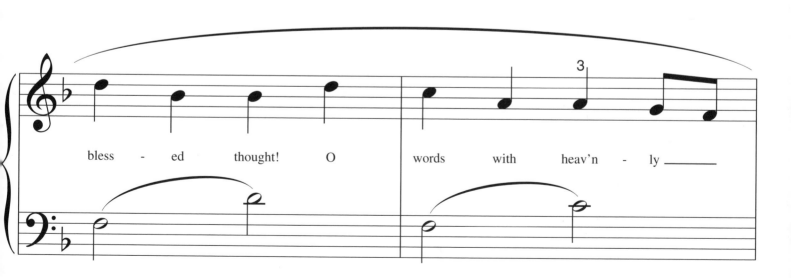

I SURRENDER ALL

Words by J.W. VAN DEVENTER
Music by W.S. WEEDEN
Arranged by Phillip Keveren

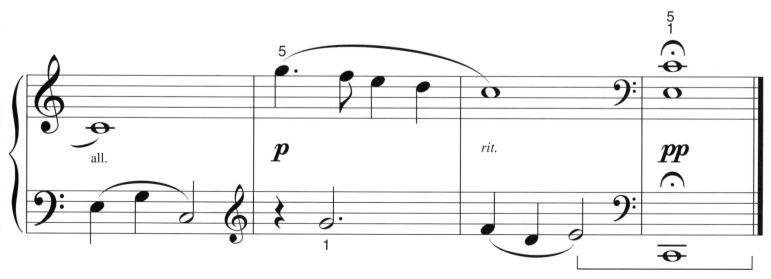

LOVE DIVINE, ALL LOVES EXCELLING

Words by CHARLES WESLEY
Music by JOHN ZUNDEL
Arranged by Phillip Keveren

Moderately

REJOICE, THE LORD IS KING

Words by CHARLES WESLEY
Music by JOHN DARWALL
Arranged by Phillip Keveren

Jubilant

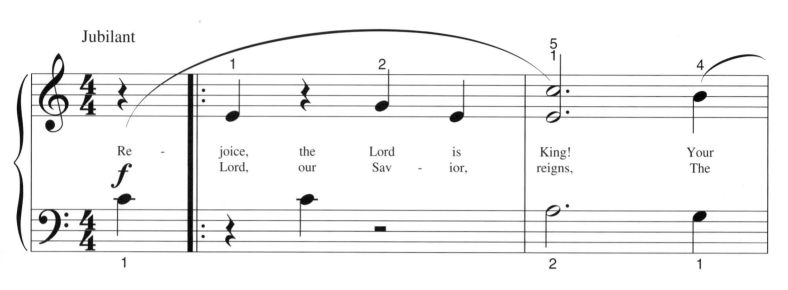

Re - joice, the Lord is King! Your
Lord, our Lord Sav - ior, reigns, The

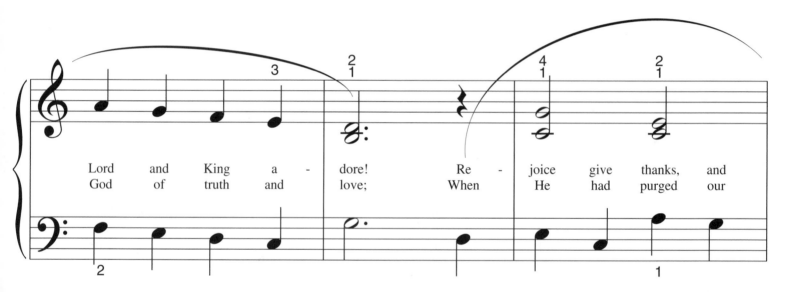

Lord and King a - dore! Re - joice give thanks, and
God of King truth and love; When He had purged our

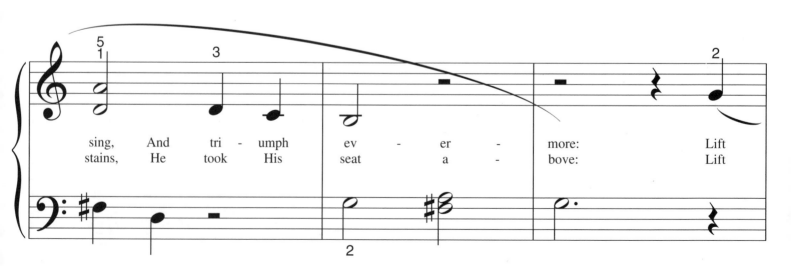

sing, And tri - umph ev - er - more: Lift
stains, He took His seat a - bove: Lift

33

34

keys of death and hell Are to our Je - sus

cresc.

f

giv'n: Lift up your heart, lift

p cresc.

up your voice! Re - joice, a - gain I

rit.

say, re - joice!

f

PRAISE GOD, FROM WHOM ALL BLESSINGS FLOW

Words by THOMAS KEN
Music attributed to LOUIS BOURGEOIS
Arranged by Phillip Keveren

OPEN MY EYES, THAT I MAY SEE

Words and Music by CLARA H. SCOTT
Arranged by Phillip Keveren

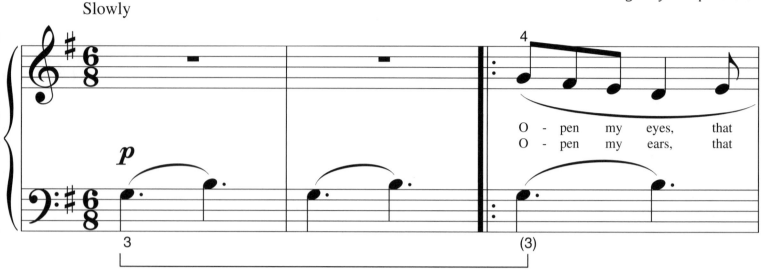

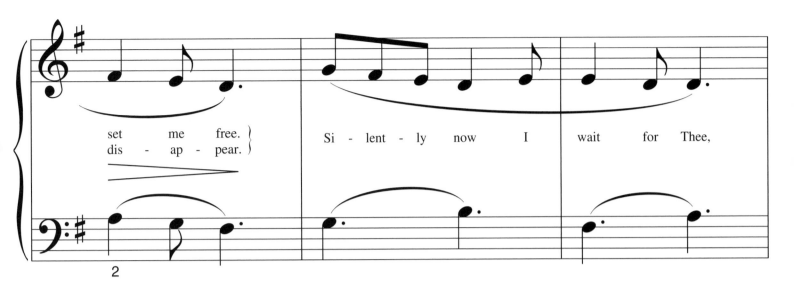

set me free.
dis - ap - pear.

Si - lent - ly now I wait for Thee,

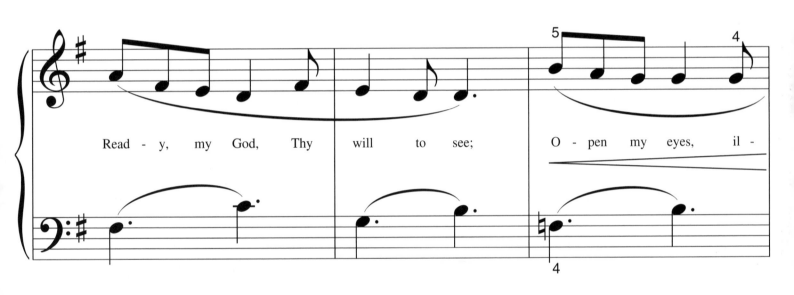

Read - y, my God, Thy will to see; O - pen my eyes, il -

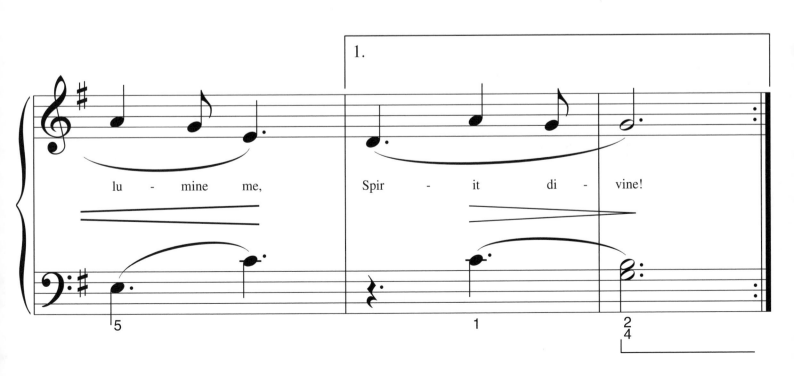

1.

lu - mine me, Spir - it di - vine!

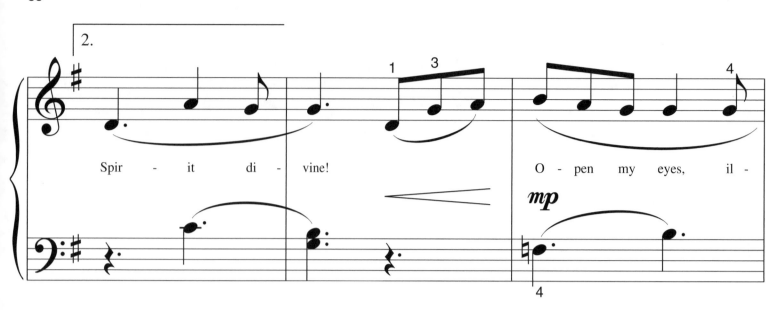

Spir - it di - vine! O - pen my eyes, il-

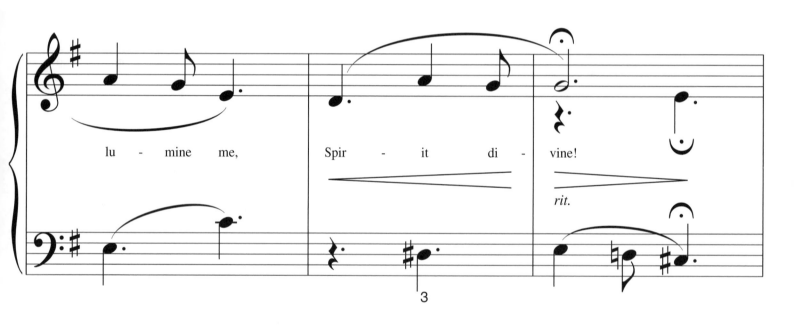

lu - mine me, Spir - it di - vine!

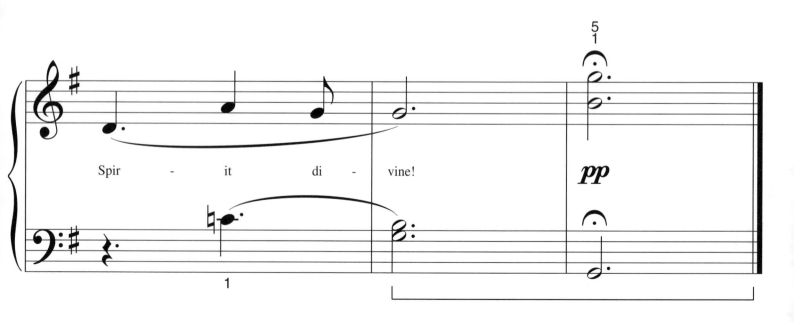

Spir - it di - vine!

THE OLD RUGGED CROSS

Words and Music by REV. GEORGE BENNARD
Arranged by Phillip Keveren

40

PRAISE TO THE LORD, THE ALMIGHTY

Words by JOACHIM NEANDER
Translated by CATHERINE WINKWORTH
Music from *Erneuerten Gesangbuch*
Arranged by Phillip Keveren

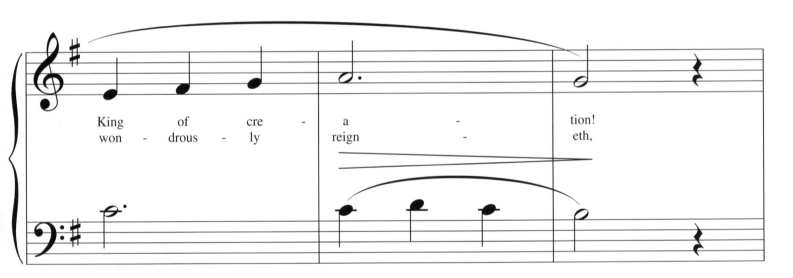

43

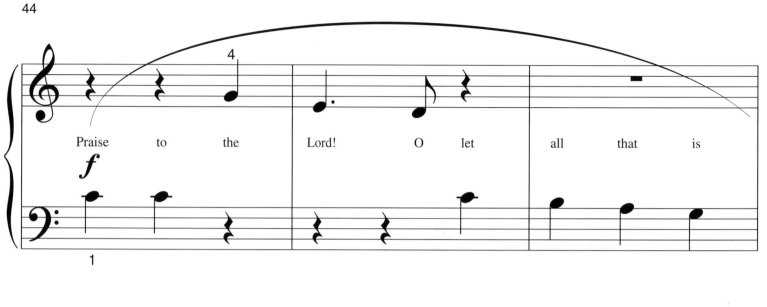

Praise to the Lord! O let all that is

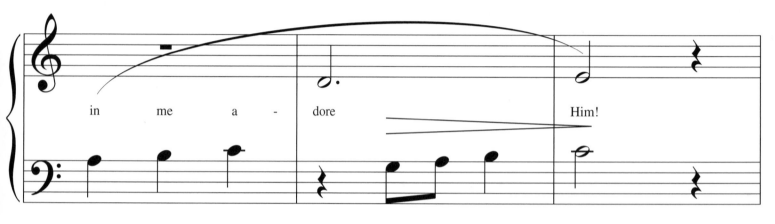

in me a - dore Him!

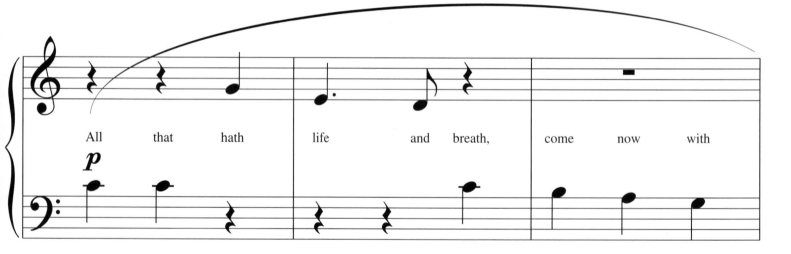

All that hath life and breath, come now with

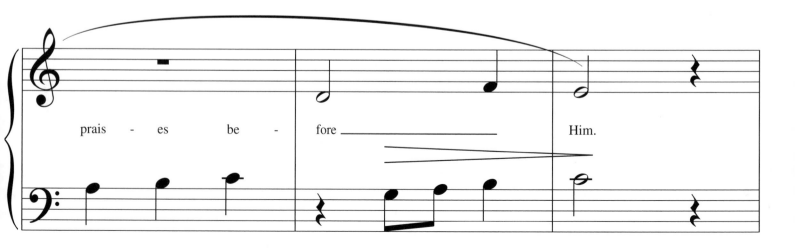

prais - es be - fore _____ Him.

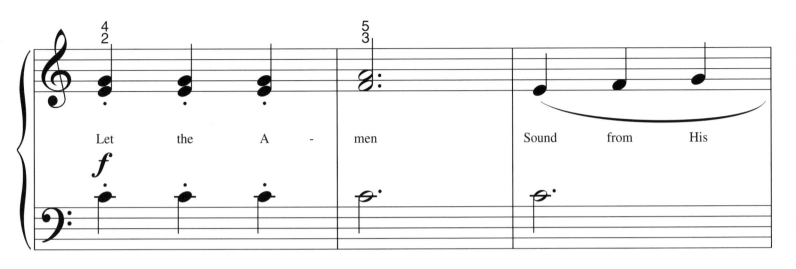

Let the A - men Sound from His

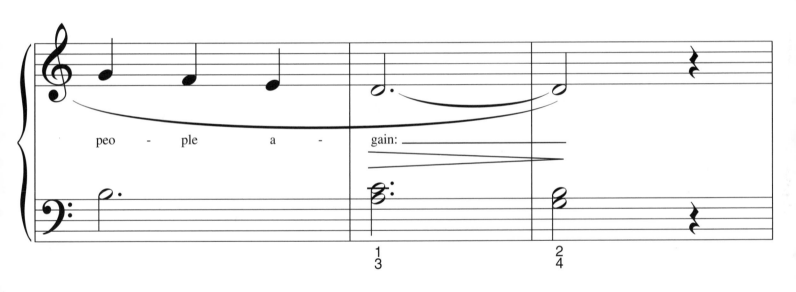

peo - ple a - gain:

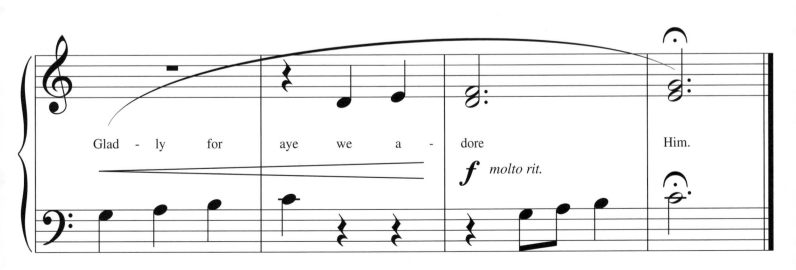

Glad - ly for aye we a - dore Him.

WE GATHER TOGETHER

Words from *Nederlandtsch Gedenckclanck*
Translated by THEODORE BAKER
Netherlands Folk Melody
Adapted by EDWARD KREMSER
Arranged by Phillip Keveren

Gently

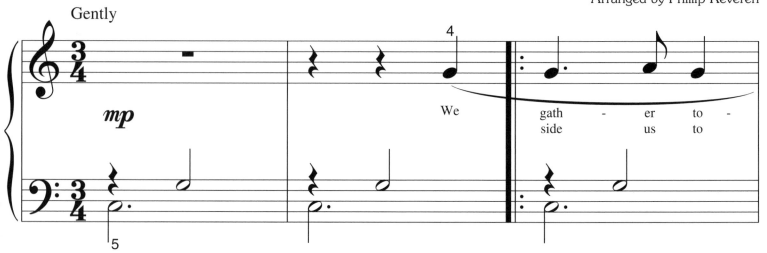

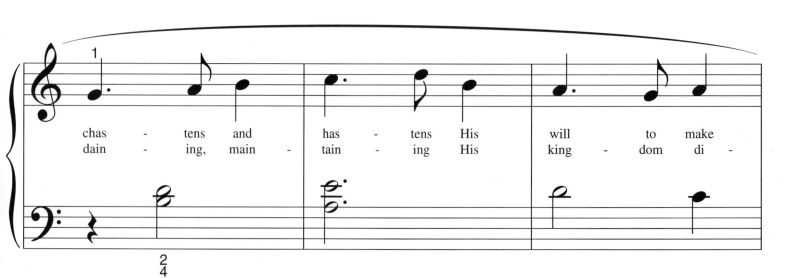

48

SOFTLY AND TENDERLY

Words and Music by WILL L. THOMPSON
Arranged by Phillip Keveren

50

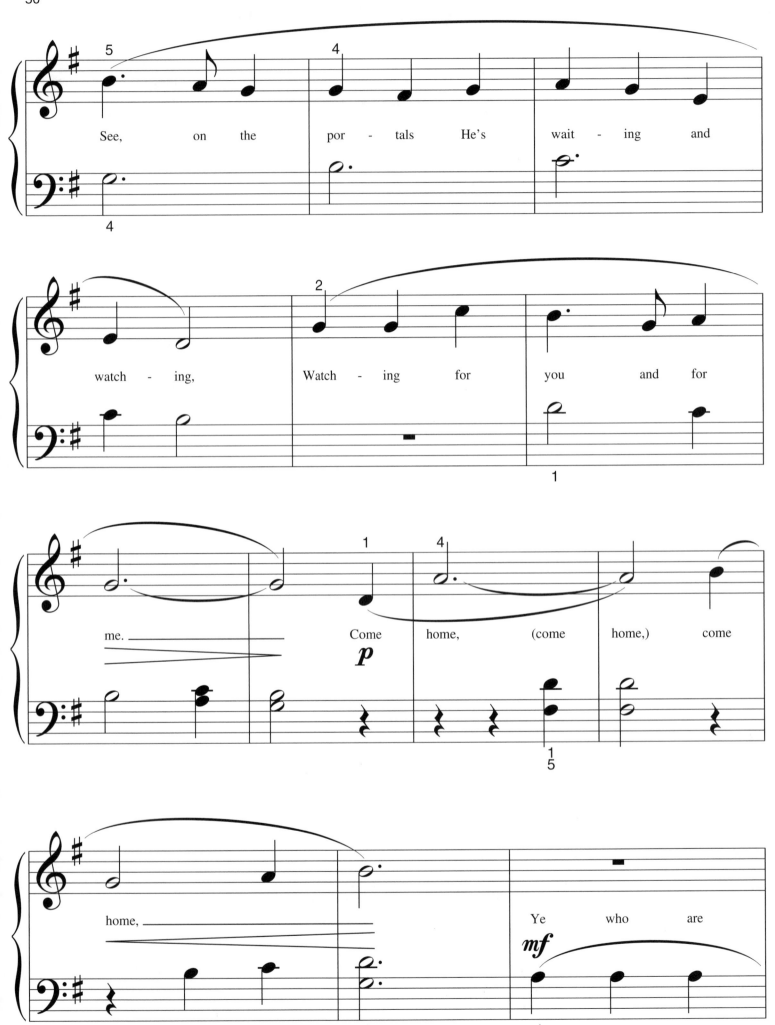

STAND UP, STAND UP FOR JESUS

Words by GEORGE DUFFIELD, JR.
Music by GEORGE J. WEBB
Arranged by Phillip Keveren

54

THIS IS MY FATHER'S WORLD

Words by MALTBIE D. BABCOCK
Music by FRANKLIN L. SHEPPARD
Arranged by Phillip Keveren

All Hail the Power of Jesus' Name

1. All hail the pow'r of Jesus' name!
    Let angels prostrate fall;
    Bring forth the royal diadem,
    And crown Him Lord of all;
    Bring forth the royal diadem,
    And crown Him Lord of all.

2. Ye chosen seed of Israel's race,
    Ye ransomed from the fall,
    Hail Him who saves you by His grace,
    And crown Him Lord of all.
    Hail Him who saves you by His grace,
    And crown Him Lord of all.

3. Sinners, whose love can ne'er forget
    The wormword and the gall,
    Go spread your trophies at His feet,
    And crown Him Lord of all.
    Go spread your trophies at His feet,
    And crown Him Lord of all.

4. Let ev'ry kindred, ev'ry tribe
    On this terrestrial ball
    To Him all majesty ascribe,
    And crown Him Lord of all.
    To Him all majesty ascribe,
    And crown Him Lord of all.

5. Crown Him, ye martyrs of your God,
    Who from His altar call,
    Extol the Stem of Jesse's Rod,
    And crown Him Lord of all.
    Extol the Stem of Jesse's Rod,
    And crown Him Lord of all.

6. Oh that with yonder sacred throng
    We at His feet may fall.
    We'll join the everlasting song
    And crown Him Lord of all.
    We'll join the everlasting song
    And crown Him Lord of all.

Be Still, My Soul

1. Be still, my soul! The Lord is on thy side;
    Bear patiently the cross of grief or pain;
    Leave to thy God to order and provide;
    In ev'ry change He faithful will remain.
    Be still, my soul! Thy best, thy heav'nly Friend
    Through thorny ways leads to a joyful end.

2. Be still, my soul! Thy God doth undertake
    To guide the future as He has the past.
    Thy hope, thy confidence let nothing shake;
    All now mysterious shall be bright at last.
    Be still, my soul! The waves and winds still know
    His voice who ruled them while He dwelt below.

3. Be still, my soul! The hour is hast'ning on
    When we shall be forever with the Lord,
    When disappointment, grief and fear are gone,
    Sorrow forgot, love's purest joys restored.
    Be still, my soul! When change and tears are past,
    All safe and blessed we shall meet at last.

Be Thou My Vision

1. Be Thou my vision, O Lord of my heart;
   Naught be all else to me, save that Thou art;
   Thou my best thought, by day or by night,
   Waking or sleeping, Thy presence my light.

2. Riches I heed not, nor vain, empty praise.
   Thou mine inheritance, now and always;
   Thou and Thou only, first in my heart,
   Great God of heaven, my treasure Thou art.

3. Be Thou my wisdom, and Thou my true word;
   I ever with Thee and Thou with me, Lord:
   Thou my great Father, I Thy true son,
   Thou in me dwelling, and I with Thee one.

4. High King of heaven, when vict'ry is won,
   May I reach heaven's joys, bright heaven's sun!
   Heart of my heart, whatever befall,
   Still be my vision, O Ruler of all.

The Church's One Foundation

1. The Church's one foundation is Jesus Christ her Lord;
   She is His new creation by water and the word:
   From heav'n He came and sought her to be
      His holy bride;
   With His own blood He bought her, and for her life
      He died.

2. Elect from ev'ry nation, yet one o'er all the earth,
   Her charter of salvation, one Lord, one faith, one birth;
   One holy name she blesses, partakes one holy food,
   And to one hope she presses, with ev'ry grace endued.

3. Though with a scornful wonder men see her
      sore oppressed,
   By schisms rent asunder, by heresies distressed;
   Yet saints their watch are keeping, their cry goes up,
      "How long?"
   And soon the night of weeping shall be the morn of song.

4. Mid toil and tribulation, and tumult of her war
   She waits the consummation of peace forevermore;
   Till with the vision glorious her longing eyes are blessed,
   And the great Church victorious shall be the
      Church at rest.

5. Yet she on earth hath union with God, the Three in One,
   And mystic sweet communion with those
      whose rest is won.
   O happy ones and holy! Lord, give us grace that we
   Like them, the meek and lowly, on high may
      dwell with Thee.

Come, Thou Fount of Every Blessing

1. Come, Thou Fount of ev'ry blessing,
   Tune my heart to sing Thy grace;
   Streams of mercy, never ceasing,
   Call for songs of loudest praise.
   Teach me some melodious sonnet,
   Sung by flaming tongues above;
   Praise His name, I'm fixed upon it,
   Name of God's redeeming love.

2. Here I raise mine Ebenezer;
   Hither by Thy help I'm come;
   And I hope, by Thy good pleasure,
   Safely to arrive at home.
   Jesus sought me when a stranger,
   Wand'ring from the fold of God;
   He, to rescue me from danger,
   Bought me with His precious blood.

3. O to grace how great a debtor
   Daily I'm constrained to be!
   Let Thy goodness, like a fetter,
   Bind my wand'ring heart to Thee.
   Prone to wander, Lord, I feel it,
   Prone to leave the God I love;
   Here's my heart, O take and seal it,
   Seal it for Thy courts above.

Come, Thou Long-Expected Jesus

1. Come, Thou long-expected Jesus,
   Born to set Thy people free;
   From our fears and sins release us;
   Let us find our rest in Thee.
   Israel's strength and consolation,
   Hope of all the earth Thou art;
   Dear desire of ev'ry nation,
   Joy of ev'ry longing heart.

2. Born Thy people to deliver,
   Born a child and yet a king.
   Born to reign in us forever,
   Now Thy gracious kingdom bring.
   By Thine own eternal Spirit
   Rule in all our hearts alone;
   By Thine all-sufficient merit
   Raise us to Thy glorious throne.

Fairest Lord Jesus

1. Fairest Lord Jesus, Ruler of all nature,
   O Thou of God and man the Son:
   Thee will I cherish, Thee will I honor,
   Thou, my soul's glory, joy, and crown.

2. Fair are the meadows, fairer still the woodlands,
   Robed in the blooming garb of spring:
   Jesus is fairer, Jesus is purer,
   Who makes the woeful heart to sing.

3. Fair is the sunshine, fairer still the moonlight,
   And all the twinkling, starry host:
   Jesus shines brighter, Jesus shines purer
   Than all the angels heav'n can boast.

4. Beautiful Savior! Lord of the nations!
   Son of God and Son of Man!
   Glory and honor, praise, adoration,
   Now and forevermore be Thine!

He Leadeth Me

1. He leadeth me! O blessed thought!
   O words with heav'nly comfort fraught!
   Whate'er I do, where'er I be,
   Still 'tis God's hand that leadeth me!
   Refrain:
   He leadeth me, He leadeth me,
   By His own hand He leadeth me.
   His faithful foll'wer, I would be,
   For by His hand He leadeth me.

2. Sometimes 'mid scenes of deepest gloom,
   Sometimes where Eden's bowers bloom,
   By waters still, o'er troubled sea,
   Still 'tis God's hand that leadeth me.
   Refrain

3. Lord, I would clasp Thy hand in mine,
   Nor ever murmur nor repine;
   Content, whatever lot I see,
   Since 'tis Thy hand that leadeth me.
   Refrain

4. And when my task on earth is done,
   When, by Thy grace, the vict'ry's won,
   E'en death's cold wave I will not flee,
   Since God through Jordan leadeth me.
   Refrain

I Surrender All

1. All to Jesus I surrender,
   All to Him I freely give;
   I will ever love and trust Him,
   In His presence daily live.
   Refrain:
   I surrender all, I surrender all,
   All to Thee, my blessed Savior,
   I surrender all.

2. All to Jesus I surrender,
   Humbly at His feet I bow;
   Worldly pleasures all forsaken,
   Take me, Jesus, take me now.
   Refrain

3. All to Jesus I surrender,
   Make me, Savior, wholly Thine;
   Let me feel the Holy Spirit,
   Truly know that Thou art mine.
   Refrain

4. All to Jesus I surrender,
   Lord, I give myself to Thee;
   Fill me with Thy love and power,
   Let Thy blessing fall on me.
   Refrain

5. All to Jesus I surrender,
   Now I feel the sacred flame;
   O the joy of full salvation!
   Glory, glory to His Name!
   Refrain

Love Divine, All Loves Excelling

1. Love divine, all loves excelling,
   Joy of heav'n, to earth come down;
   Fix in us Thy humble dwelling,
   All Thy faithful mercies crown.
   Jesus, Thou art all compassion,
   Pure, unbounded love Thou art;
   Visit us with Thy salvation,
   Enter ev'ry trembling heart.

2. Breathe, O breathe Thy loving Spirit
   Into ev'ry troubled breast!
   Let us all in Thee inherit,
   Let us find that promised rest.
   Take away the love of sinning,
   Alpha and Omega be;
   End of faith, as its beginning,
   Set our hearts at liberty.

3. Come, almighty to deliver,
   Let us all Thy life receive;
   Suddenly return and never,
   Nevermore Thy temples leave.
   Thee we would be always blessing,
   Serve Thee as Thy hosts above,
   Pray, and praise Thee without ceasing,
   Glory in Thy perfect love.

4. Finish, then, Thy new creation;
   Pure and spotless let us be.
   Let us see Thy great salvation
   Perfectly restored in Thee;
   Changed from glory into glory,
   Till in heav'n we take our place,
   Till we cast our crowns before Thee,
   Lost in wonder, love, and praise.

Nearer, My God, To Thee

1. Nearer, my God, to Thee, nearer to Thee!
   E'en though it be a cross that raiseth me;
   Still all my song shall be, nearer, my God, to Thee,
   Nearer, my God, to Thee, Nearer to Thee!

2. Though like the wanderer, the sun gone down,
   Darkness be over me, my rest a stone;
   Yet in my dreams I'd be nearer, my God, to Thee,
   Nearer, my God, to Thee, Nearer to Thee!

3. There let the way appear, steps unto heav'n;
   All that Thou sendest me in mercy giv'n,
   Angels to beckon me nearer, my God, to Thee,
   Nearer, my God, to Thee, Nearer to Thee!

4. Then, with my waking thoughts bright with Thy praise,
   Out of my stony griefs Bethel I'll raise;
   So by my woes to be nearer, my God, to Thee,
   Nearer, my God, to Thee, Nearer to Thee!

5. Or, if on joyful wing cleaving the sky,
   Sun, moon and stars forgot, upward I'll fly,
   Still all my song shall be, nearer, my God, to Thee,
   Nearer, my God, to Thee, Nearer to Thee!

The Old Rugged Cross

1. On a hill far away stood an old rugged cross,
    The emblem of suff'ring and shame;
    And I love that old cross, where the dearest and best
    For a world of lost sinners was slain.
    Refrain:
    So I'll cherish the old rugged cross,
    Till my trophies at last I lay down;
    I will cling to the old rugged cross,
    And exchange it some day for a crown.

2. O that old rugged cross, so despised by the world,
    Has a wondrous attraction for me;
    For the dear Lamb of God left His glory above
    To bear it to dark Calvary.
    Refrain

3. In that old rugged cross, stained with blood so divine,
    A wondrous beauty I see,
    For 'twas on that old cross Jesus suffered and died,
    To pardon and sanctify me.
    Refrain

4. To the old rugged cross I will ever be true;
    Its shame and reproach gladly bear;
    Then He'll call me someday to my home far away,
    Where His glory forever I'll share.
    Refrain

Open My Eyes, That I May See

1. Open my eyes, that I may see
    Glimpses of truth Thou hast for me;
    Place in my hands the wonderful key
    That shall unclasp and set me free.
    Refrain:
    Silently now I wait for Thee,
    Ready, my God, Thy will to see;
    Open my eyes, illumine me,
    Spirit divine!

2. Open my ears, that I may hear
    Voices of truth Thou sendest clear;
    And while the wave-notes fall on my ear,
    Everything false will disappear.
    Refrain

3. Open my mouth, and let me bear,
    Gladly the warm truth everywhere;
    Open my heart and let me prepare
    Love with Thy children thus to share.
    Refrain

4. Open my mind, that I may read
    More of Thy love in word and deed.
    What shall I fear while yet Thou dost lead?
    Only for light from Thee I plead.
    Refrain

Praise God, From Whom All Blessings Flow

Praise God, from whom all blessings flow;
Praise Him, all creatures here below;
Praise Him above, ye heav'nly host;
Praise Father, Son and Holy Ghost. Amen.

Praise to the Lord, The Almighty

1. Praise to the Lord, the Almighty, the King of creation!
   O my soul, praise Him, for He is thy health and salvation!
   All ye who hear, now to His temple draw near;
   Join me in glad adoration!

2. Praise to the Lord, who o'er all things so
      wondrously reigneth,
   Shelters thee under His wings, yes, so gently sustaineth!
   Hast thou not seen how all thy longings have been
   Granted in what He ordaineth?

3. Praise to the Lord, who doth prosper thy work and
      defend thee;
   Surely His goodness and mercy here daily attend thee.
   Ponder anew what the Almighty can do,
   If with His love He befriend thee.

4. Praise to the Lord! O let all that is in me adore Him!
   All that hath life and breath, come now with praises
      before Him.
   Let the Amen sound from His people again:
   Gladly for aye we adore Him.

Rejoice, The Lord Is King

1. Rejoice, the Lord is King! Your Lord and King adore!
   Rejoice, give thanks and sing, and triumph evermore:
   Lift up your heart, lift up your voice!
   Rejoice, again I say, rejoice!

2. The Lord, our Savior, reigns, the God of truth and love;
   When He had purged our stains, He took His seat above:
   Lift up your heart, lift up your voice!
   Rejoice, again I say, rejoice!

3. His kingdom cannot fail, He rules o'er earth and heav'n;
   The keys of death and hell are to our Jesus giv'n:
   Lift up your heart, lift up your voice!
   Rejoice, again I say, rejoice!

4. Rejoice in glorious hope! For Christ, the Judge, shall come
   To glorify the saints for their eternal home:
   Lift up your heart, lift up your voice;
   Rejoice, again I say, rejoice!

Softly and Tenderly

1. Softly and tenderly Jesus is calling,
   Calling for you and for me;
   See, on the portals He's waiting and watching,
   Watching for you and for me.
   Refrain:
   Come home, come home,
   Ye who are weary, come home;
   Earnestly, tenderly, Jesus is calling,
   Calling, O sinner, come home!

2. Why should we tarry when Jesus is pleading,
   Pleading for you and for me?
   Why should we linger and heed not His mercies,
   Mercies for you and for me?
   Refrain

3. Time is now fleeting, the moments are passing,
   Passing from you and from me;
   Shadows are gathering, death's night is coming,
   Coming for you and for me.
   Refrain

4. O, for the wonderful love He has promised,
   Promised for you and for me!
   Though we have sinned, He has mercy and pardon,
   Pardon for you and for me.
   Refrain

Stand Up, Stand Up for Jesus

1. Stand up, stand up for Jesus, ye soldiers of the cross;
   Lift high His royal banner, it must not suffer loss;
   From vict'ry unto vict'ry His army shall He lead,
   Till ev'ry foe is vanquished and Christ is Lord indeed.

2. Stand up, stand up for Jesus, the trumpet call obey;
   Forth to the mighty conflict in this His glorious day.
   Ye that are men, now serve Him against
       unnumbered foes;
   Let courage rise with danger, and strength to
       strength oppose.

3. Stand up, stand up for Jesus, stand in His
       strength alone;
   The arm of flesh will fail you, ye dare not trust
       your own.
   Put on the gospel armor, each piece put on
       with prayer;
   Where duty calls or danger, be never wanting there.

4. Stand up, stand up for Jesus, the strife will not be long;
   This day the noise of battle, the next, the victor's song.
   To those who overcometh, a crown of life shall be;
   He with the King of Glory shall reign eternally.

This Is My Father's World

1. This is my Father's world, and to my list'ning ears
   All nature sings, and round me rings the music
      of the spheres.
   This is my Father's world: I rest me in the thought
   Of rocks and trees, of skies and seas
   His hand the wonders wrought.

2. This is my Father's world, the birds their carols raise,
   The morning light, the lily white, declare their
      Maker's praise.
   This is my Father's world: He shines in all that's fair;
   In the rustling grass I hear Him pass,
   He speaks to me ev'rywhere.

3. This is my Father's world, O let me ne'er forget
   That though the wrong seems oft so strong,
      God is the Ruler yet.
   This is my Father's world: The battle is not done;
   Jesus who died shall be satisfied,
   And earth and heav'n be one.

We Gather Together

1. We gather together to ask the Lord's blessing;
   He chastens and hastens His will to make known;
   The wicked oppressing now cease from distressing.
   Sing praises to His Name; He forgets not His own.

2. Beside us to guide us, our God with us joining,
   Ordaining, maintaining His kingdom divine;
   So from the beginning the fight we were winning;
   Thou, Lord, wast at our side, all glory be Thine!

3. We all do extol Thee, Thou Leader triumphant,
   And pray that Thou still our Defender wilt be.
   Let Thy congregation escape tribulation;
   Thy Name be ever praised! O Lord, make us free!